WILD BEARS!

PANDA

**Text and Photographs by
Tom and Pat Leeson**

BLACKBIRCH PRESS, INC.

WOODBRIDGE, CONNECTICUT

Published by Blackbirch Press, Inc.
260 Amity Road
Woodbridge, CT 06525

Email: staff@blackbirch.com
Web site: www.blackbirch.com

Printed in the United States

10 9 8 7 6 5 4 3

All photographs ©Tom and Pat Leeson, except pages 16 and 17 (left): ©China Span.

Library of Congress Cataloging-in-Publication Data
Leeson, Tom.
Panda / text & photographs by Tom & Pat Leeson
        p. cm. — (Wild bears!)
    Includes bibliographical references.
    Summary: Describes the physical appearance, habits, hunting and mating behaviors, family life, and life cycle of giant pandas.
    ISBN 1-56711-341-9
    1. Giant panda—Juvenile literature. [1. Giant panda. 2. Pandas.] I. Leeson, Pat. II. Title.

QL737.C214 L46 2000
599.789—dc21   99-059464

Contents

Introduction

Pandas have always fascinated humans. In the past, many people thought pandas had special powers and healing abilities. Ancient Chinese emperors kept pandas as pets in their gardens.

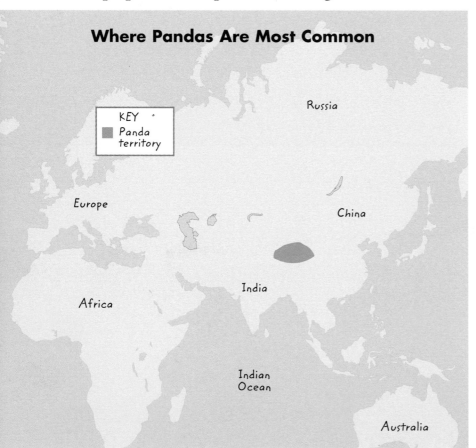

Where Pandas Are Most Common

KEY
Panda territory

Russia

Europe

China

Africa

India

Indian Ocean

Australia

If you have ever seen a giant panda in a zoo, you are very lucky. These bears are so rare that very few zoos in North America have them. Today, these endangered bears live only in the bamboo forests of central China. Scientists who study pandas think that there are only about 1,000 of these bears still living in the wild.

Opposite top and bottom: Giant pandas have fascinated people for many centuries. They only live in the bamboo forests on the steep mountain slopes of central China.

Pandas have moved to higher and higher living quarters as humans have moved into the bears' habitat. Now, pandas spend their days on the steep mountain slopes of central China. They spend most of the year at elevations between 5,000 to 12,000 feet (1,525 to 3,600 meters). In winter, giant pandas migrate (travel) down the mountain slopes to lower, warmer areas.

The Panda Body

In shape and size, pandas look like most other bears. Their unusual coloring sometimes reminds people of raccoons. Pandas' bodies are covered with white and black fur. They have black fur around their eyes, ears, legs, and shoulders. Pandas also have white, stubby tails.

Giant pandas have thick, woolly fur that protects them from harsh weather. Their mountain habitat gets cold and snowy in the winter. Even summer weather can be damp and cool. Panda fur is slightly oily to prevent water from seeping through to the bear's skin.

While "giant" is part of a panda's name, it is certainly not a giant creature in the animal world. The average adult panda is about 5 feet (1.35 meters) long and weighs about 200 pounds (90 kilograms). Pandas, in fact, are only 2 to 3 times bigger than a large dog.

Top: Because of their coloring, many people think that pandas look a lot like raccoons.
Bottom: Pandas have slightly oily fur, which prevents water from reaching their skin.

Pandas look somewhat clumsy. They have a waddling walk, but when they are frightened they are able to trot like a horse. Because they have sharp claws, they are also able to climb trees easily.

Pandas are crepuscular animals. That means they are active during twilight—mostly in the morning and evening. They tend to nap 2 to 4 hours at a time during the afternoon. Pandas are able to sleep on their backs, stomachs—or even draped over a tree limb. Sometimes they will even snore!

Top left: Sharp claws help pandas climb trees.
Top right: Giant pandas are about 5 feet tall (1.35 meters).
Below: Pandas are able to sleep in almost any position.

Special Features

One of the giant panda's unique features is a special "thumb" pad on its front paws. Like monkeys and humans, it can use this thumb to grasp and hold objects between its thumb and toe pads. But, unlike humans or apes—whose thumbs are a modified fifth finger—the thumb on a panda is an extension of its wrist bones.

A panda uses its thumb pad to hold a bamboo stalk.
Inset: The thumbs on a panda's paws are actually extensions of its wrist bones.

These extensions work like sixth fingers. With this thumb, a panda can easily grab and hold bamboo, which is its main source of food.

Unlike most bears, pandas have well-developed molars. These large teeth are flattened on top so that pandas can chew through tough bamboo shoots. Pandas also have strong jaw muscles that allow them to crush hard stalks.

Pandas do not hibernate (sleep though the winter) like North American black bears and grizzly bears. Even though there is ice, snow, and cold weather where they live in China, pandas stay awake and search for food all winter long. Some scientists believe this is because bamboo does not provide enough nutrition for pandas to sleep for several months without eating.

Pandas have excellent hearing and a good sense of smell. These senses make up for their poor eyesight. Sometimes pandas walk past tasty bamboo shoots because they simply do not see them!

Strong jaw muscles and flattened teeth allow pandas to chew tough bamboo.

Social Life

Like many mammals, giant pandas are shy and solitary (they prefer to live alone). They communicate, or "speak," to other pandas by marking their territories with their scents. Sometimes, they will scratch the bark of trees with their front claws. Other times, they will leave scent marks by spraying a bush or rock with urine. Often, giant pandas will rub their scent glands, which are located on their bottoms, against a tree or boulder.

These scent markers tell other pandas that someone else already lives in that area of forest. Using these markers and scents, pandas are mostly able to avoid one another, which prevents a fight over the same territory.

Pandas leave scent marks by scratching trees with their front claws.

Some scientists think that a panda's bold markings also play a major role in how the bears get along with one another. Their highly noticeable black-and-white coats may help pandas to spot one another easily in the wild. This can help pandas to find mates during breeding season, and makes it easier to avoid other pandas during the rest of the year.

Bold markings may help pandas locate one another during mating season.

Food

Bamboo makes up about 95% of a panda's diet. The average panda will usually spend 10 to 16 hours each day eating, and will consume between 20 to 70 pounds (10 to 38 kilograms) of bamboo. In one year, a panda will eat more than 12 tons of bamboo! Pandas need to eat this much because bamboo provides very little nourishment. Pandas only digest about 20% of the bamboo they eat. Even though they are mainly vegetarian, they have almost the same digestive system as carnivores (meat-eaters).

Pandas prefer tender, young bamboo shoots, but they also eat bamboo stems and leaves. While they do not like the older, woody bamboo stalks, pandas will chew these tough stems when there is little food available.

Top and bottom: A panda's diet consists almost entirely of bamboo. To get enough nourishment, pandas need to eat about 12 tons of bamboo per year.

Above left: In captivity, pandas are sometimes fed apples. **Above right:** Pandas often lie down when they eat.

Giant pandas will also eat wildflowers and grasses. Sometimes they even hunt for fish, small rodents, or honey. In zoos, they are fed apples and carrots, along with bamboo.

There are many different species of bamboo plants, but pandas eat only 25 kinds. Occasionally, in large areas, a species of bamboo that many pandas feed on will flower (produce seeds) and die off. Although new bamboo plants begin to grow within a year, it can take up to 15 years for the plants to grow large enough to support the same number of pandas they once fed. The lack of bamboo can seriously hurt the panda population.

The Mating Game

While pandas spend most of their time alone, adults—those aged 4 years and older—will look for a mate between March and May. Female pandas make moaning sounds and bleat (call) like sheep when they are ready to mate. Sometimes this will attract several males, but the female will only mate with the strongest and most aggressive male. After mating, both pandas return to their lives alone. Pandas only mate once every 2 or 3 years.

Male and female pandas only come together during mating season.

Female pandas will only mate once every 2 or 3 years.

Raising Young

After about 5 months, usually during August or September, a very small baby is born. Most pandas are born in a hollow tree or cave. A newborn weighs only 3 to 5 ounces (85–142 grams). A panda cub is born blind, and has a thin coat of white fur over its pink skin. Usually only 1 or 2 cubs are born at a time. If 2 cubs are born, it is very rare that both will survive.

A mother panda often cradles her cub to her chest.

Like human mothers, a mother panda spends time bathing and feeding her young. She frequently licks her cub to keep it clean. A mother panda must keep both her cub and her den clean so they won't attract hungry leopards or wild dogs. A mother panda sometimes nurses her baby cub for 12 to 14 hours per day. She often picks up her cub and cradles it to her chest, just like a human mother does.

Right: A cub's fur fills in and darkens a bit as the panda gets older.
Below: A mother panda spends most of her day cleaning and nursing her cub.

Cubs learn to walk and play a couple of months after birth.

After about a week, the white hair on a cub's ears, shoulders, legs, and eyes starts to turn gray. After 3 weeks, this gray hair turns black, and a young cub begins to look more like its adult parents. A cub's eyes open at about 6 weeks. It will still be a couple of weeks, however, before it can keep both eyes open, and another month before its vision becomes clear.

Cubs begin to walk 3 to 4 months after birth. By the time they are 8 or 9 months old, they eat mostly bamboo. At 1 year, cubs weigh roughly 55 to 75 pounds (25 to 34 kilograms).

A cub stays with its mother for about 18 months.

Over the next 5 to 6 months, the growing panda will gain another 40 to 50 pounds (18 to 23 kilograms). By 18 months, the cubs are mature and experienced enough to leave their mothers and live on their own. In the wild, giant pandas may live from 20 to 25 years.

No Less a Panda

In and around the same mountain area of Asia where giant pandas live, a smaller animal shares the territory. The red panda, or lesser panda, is actually related to both the giant panda and the raccoon families. This animal is about the same size as a raccoon, but is a rusty-brown color. It has a long, bushy tail, and small, pointed ears.

The red panda is a nocturnal animal. This means it is active mostly from dusk to dawn. It spends the night searching for food. Like the giant panda, the red panda especially likes to eat bamboo. Unlike the giant panda, it will also eat plants, roots, eggs, and small mammals. During the day, red pandas rest in the branches of tall trees.

Pandas and Humans

Giant pandas are one of the most endangered animals in the world. Several thousand years ago, they were much more common and lived throughout southern and eastern China. They were even found as far south in Asia as Vietnam, Laos, and Myanmar (formerly Burma).

But over time, the climate in Asia began to change. Eventually, bamboo did not grow in as many locations as it once had. At the

Biologists study and breed pandas at the Wolong Preserve in China.

same time, many more people began to live in what was left of the panda's bamboo forests. These newcomers cleared bamboo from the forests so they could farm. They grew corn, potatoes, and beans—among other crops. Because this human activity destroyed bamboo forests, the food supply for pandas shrank. There was almost no place for pandas to live. Some pandas were also killed by traps that had been set for other animals.

Many people today are working to save giant pandas. The Chinese government has established several large panda preserves and centers where scientists can help these endangered creatures. In the United States, some zoos try to breed pandas. These zoos also contribute to panda research and preservation.

Preserves provide pandas with bamboo and protect them from human threats.

Pandas cannot survive without respect and cooperation from humans.

With help from humans, pandas have a chance to once again establish themselves in stable bamboo forests. But without human cooperation, these beautiful animals have little chance of surviving in the future.

Panda Facts

Name: Giant Panda, Panda bear or—in Chinese—daxiong Mao (DAH-SHWING MA-HOO)

Scientific Name: Ailuropoda melanoleuca

Shoulder Height: 25 to 32 inches (64–81 centimeters)

Body length: 4–6 feet (1.2–1.8 meters)

Tail length: 5–7 inches (13–18 centimeters)

Weight: 170–325 pounds (77–147 kilograms)

Color: Black and white

Reaches sexual maturity: 4 to 5 years

Females mate: Once every 2 to 3 years

Gestation: About 5 months

Litter size: 1 to 2 cubs, though usually only 1 cub survives

Social life: Lives alone

Favorite food: Young, tender bamboo shoots

Habitat: Forested mountains in central China

Glossary

carnivore Meat-eater.
climate The usual weather in a place.
emperor The male ruler of an empire.
endangered A plant or animal species that is in danger of becoming extinct.
habitat The place and natural conditions in which a plant or animal lives.

migrate To travel when the seasons change.
modified Changed slightly.
nutrition Food that your body uses to keep you healthy and strong.
preservation An area of land where certain living things are kept safe from injury, harm, or destruction.

For More Information

Books

Bailey, Donna. *Bears* (Animal World). Chatham, NJ: Steck Vaughn Company, 1998.
Bailey, Jill. *Project Panda* (Saving Our Species). Chatham, NJ: Steck Vaughn Company, 1990.
Barrett, Norman S. *Pandas.* Danbury, CT: Franklin Watts, 1990.
Dudley, Karen. *Giant Pandas* (Untamed World). Chatham, NJ: Raintree/Steck Vaughn, 1997.

Web Site

Giant Panda Research Station
Find information from the San Diego Wild Animal Park about panda characteristics, behavior, and conservation. Links to a live panda cam, and information about a cub born at the zoo—www.sandiegozoo.org/special/pandas

Index